ORIGIN STORIES

MYTHICAL

MONSTERS

BY
JEN BREACH

ILLUSTRATED BY
JOSHUA JANES

Rourke.

BEFORE AND DURING READING ACTIVITIES

Before Reading: *Building Background Knowledge and Vocabulary*

Building background knowledge can help children process new information and build upon what they already know. Before reading a book, it is important to tap into what children already know about the topic. This will help them develop their vocabulary and increase their reading comprehension.

Questions and Activities to Build Background Knowledge:

1. Look at the front cover of the book and read the title. What do you think this book will be about?
2. What do you already know about this topic?
3. Take a book walk and skim the pages. Look at the table of contents, photographs, captions, and bold words. Did these text features give you any information or predictions about what you will read in this book?

Vocabulary: *Vocabulary Is Key to Reading Comprehension*

Use the following directions to prompt a conversation about each word.

- Read the vocabulary words.
- What comes to mind when you see each word?
- What do you think each word means?

Vocabulary Words:
- *crone*
- *decompose*
- *folklore*
- *origin*
- *shape-shift*
- *vicious*

During Reading: *Reading for Meaning and Understanding*

To achieve deep comprehension of a book, children are encouraged to use close reading strategies. During reading, it is important to have children stop and make connections. These connections result in deeper analysis and understanding of a book.

 ## Close Reading a Text

During reading, have children stop and talk about the following:

- Any confusing parts
- Any unknown words
- Text to text, text to self, text to world connections
- The main idea in each chapter or heading

Encourage children to use context clues to determine the meaning of any unknown words. These strategies will help children learn to analyze the text more thoroughly as they read.

When you are finished reading this book, turn to the next-to-last page for **After-Reading Questions** and an **Activity**.

TABLE OF CONTENTS

SHALL I TELL YOU A STORY ABOUT MONSTERS?

Humans have always told stories like that.

About what creeps,

    or stalks,

        or lurks

           in the night.

What we tell, and the way we tell it, says more about us—about what we fear. Vampires, werewolves, and zombies have been haunting humans for ages. But where do these tales come from? These monstrous **origin** stories make it clear, the thing we are afraid of is ourselves.

But it wasn't always that way.

origin (OR-i-jin): the point where something starts

◆ VAMPIRES ◆

Blood.
You can't live without it.
Neither can vampires.

Stories about drinking human blood date back to 3100 BCE!

Vampires can pass for human. You might not recognize one who walks among you, thirsting for your blood. And the more human-like the monsters are ... the more terrifying they seem.

Almost every culture has **folklore** about blood-sucking monsters. In Spain, the **crone**-like Guaxa drinks blood through its single, long, sharp, bone-white tooth. In 16th century West Africa, iron-toothed Asanbosam waits for its blood-sucking victims in high trees.

You might think you know what a vampire is ... but it wasn't always that way.

VAMPIRE TRAITS

- Blood-sucking
- Immortal
- Sharp fangs
- Shape-shifter

GEOGRAPHIC LOCATIONS

IRELAND

EUROPE

SPAIN

WEST AFRICA

crone (krohn): ugly old woman; a witch-like woman

folklore (fohk-lawr): traditional beliefs, rituals, customs, or practices of a group of people

Stories reflect what we are afraid of. The people of 5th Century Europe were afraid of unknown diseases. A lot of the time, if someone was suffering from an unknown illness, it wasn't recognized as a disease. Instead, they called them a vampire.

Some unknown diseases have familiar symptoms. The disease porphyria can make people erupt in blisters if they go out in the sun. Vampires are also known for having a sensitivity to the sun. This common vampire trait could be left over from the sufferers of porphyria.

The Europeans of the Middle Ages also believed that vampires reached from beyond the grave. They sucked life, rather than blood. But the result was the same.

Vampire suspects were dug up. Winters were hard and it was a common season for people to die. In colder weather, buried bodies **decompose** slowly. That's why so many suspected vampires still looked "alive." To be sure they couldn't rise from the grave again, their heart and lungs were burned. Or their mouths were filled with rocks and dirt. Or a metal stake was driven through their chest. How *do* you kill a vampire? We can't be sure but the stake method stuck around!

decompose (de-kuhm-POZE): to rot or decay

Vlad the Impaler

In 1897, Irish author Bram Stoker wrote *Dracula*. He was likely influenced by Irish folklore about bloodsucking fairies and a Wallachian prince called Vlad "the Impaler" Drăculea. Drăculea means "dragon" in Wallachian. Stoker might also have heard of the professional vampire hunters of Bulgaria. They journeyed to villages with a suspected vampire problem, dug up the corpse, and decided how to fix the problem.

Dracula wasn't the first vampire novel. But it might be the most important. Stoker's ideas about vampires shaped how we think about them today. Like living in castles and sleeping in caskets during the day. Transylvania is associated with vampires simply because that's where Stoker set the story.

The Halloween vampire look comes from the 1930s movie *Dracula*.

WEREWOLVES

The full moon rises. It shines on fangs and claws. The breeze rustles thick fur.

Awooooooo!

A wolf? Or something more ...?

Werewolves are in stories dating back to 40 CE.

In folklore from all over the world, werewolves are people who transform into wolves. They hunt. They devour. The woods are not safe.

But werewolves don't always look like our modern version. In French folklore they are witches who **shape-shift** using spells. In Navajo tradition, they are healers who turned evil and shape-shift at will.

Human to animal transformations are everywhere in folklore. Such as werehyenas in Africa and werefoxes in China.

WEREWOLF TRAITS

- 🛡️ Strong
- ⏱️ Fast
- 🐺 Shape-shifter
- 😠 Lacks self-control

GEOGRAPHIC LOCATIONS

- FRANCE
- ICELAND
- GREECE
- NORWAY
- FINLAND
- SWEDEN
- DENMARK
- UNITED STATES OF AMERICA

shape-shift (shayp-shift): to change physical form

Werewolf stories are told wherever there are wolves. The tales are too old and too many to know who first came up with the legend. Wolves often ate sheep and other domestic animals. But every now and then, an animal would be so **vicious** that people thought it couldn't be a mere wolf.

Some medical conditions might have spread werewolf fear. Rabies is passed from animals to people by biting. Sufferers get very aggressive and are constantly hungry. So don't feed wild animals. Or werewolves!

vicious (VISH-uhs): savage, fierce, or dangerous

A few stories stick out as some of the first to mention werewolves. In the oldest known written piece of fiction, *The Epic of Gilgamesh*, a woman turns a man into a wolf. Humans also become wolves in stories from ancient Greek mythology and early Nordic folklore.

It wasn't just vicious wolves that made people certain that werewolves were real. It was also vicious people. Werewolf mythology tries to explain what happens when someone acts as an animal would. Once turned, they have no control. Their only thoughts are to hunt ...

and to kill.

In 16th century France, a few ruthless murderers were accused of being werewolves. Their crimes were so unthinkable, the only explanation that made sense was they were not human, but beast.

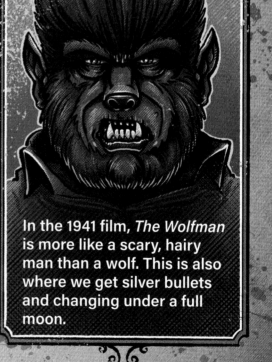

In the 1941 film, *The Wolfman* is more like a scary, hairy man than a wolf. This is also where we get silver bullets and changing under a full moon.

"Braaaaaaaains," moan the stumbling, decomposing, walking dead. A crowd of them closes in. And they just ...

keep ...

coming.

Zombies are in stories dating back to around 700 BCE!

But it wasn't always that way.

Many cultures have mythology about revenants, or people who come back from the dead. In Latin, revenant means "to come back." In Brazilian lore, there's the Dry-Corpse, who was an evil rich man in life and a walking leather-skin covered skeleton after death. In Scandinavian tales, there's the dragurs, the walking, talking, waterlogged corpses of drowned Vikings.

The mindless horde comes later...

ZOMBIE TRAITS

- 💀 Decomposing
- ∞ Relentless
- 🏃 Humanoid
- 💡 Not smart

GEOGRAPHIC LOCATIONS

WEST AFRICA

NORWAY

HAITI

SCANDINAVIA

SWEDEN

BRAZIL

HOLLYWOOD

From the 16th to 19th centuries, millions of African people were kidnapped and enslaved. Some were forced to work on plantations in Haiti. This is where the idea of a zombie originated.

According to the voodoo religion, a zombie is a living person whose soul has been stolen. They must mindlessly serve the person who turned them. For many enslaved people, this is exactly what daily life felt like. Death was seen to some as an escape. So the idea that they could die, be brought back, and enslaved again was their greatest fear.

Zombie folklore became popular in America after a white man visited Haiti and wrote a book called *The Magic Island*. In the book, the voodoo zombie is explained to readers. But it didn't take long for zombies to start looking very different in America, and for the tragic roots of the zombie to be almost forgotten.

Zombie popularity exploded in American culture with director George Romero's zombie films. He used his movies to show his fears about the problems he saw in society.

In *Night of the Living Dead* from 1968, the living people can't work together against the zombie threat. He saw American society as a group that was divided. In 1978, Romero directed *Dawn of the Dead*. In it, people hide from a zombie horde in a shopping mall. Romero was scared of mindless shopping and how having too much *stuff* was changing American culture.

Heh, humans. What will we be afraid of next?

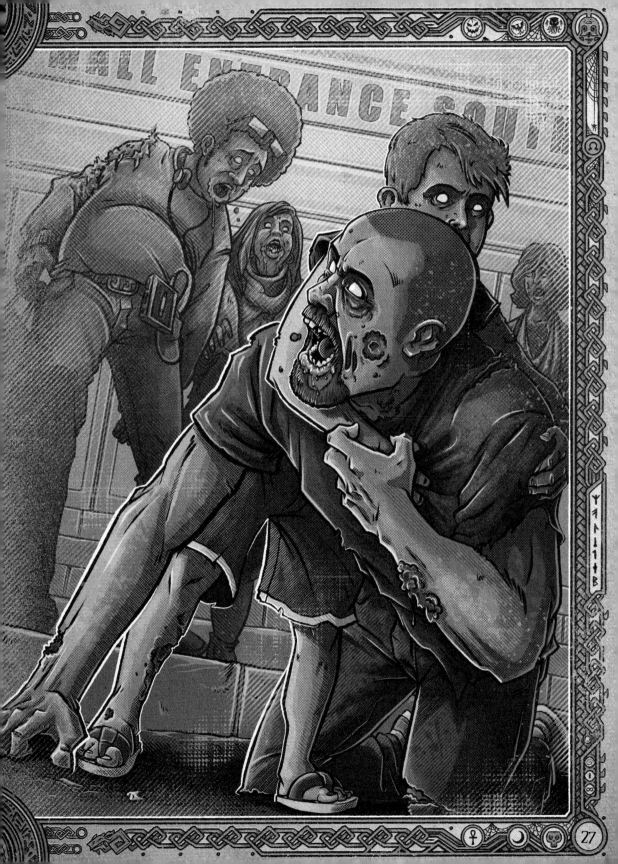

•The Next Story•

We keep writing the lore of vampires, werewolves, and zombies in movies, books, and TV. Sometimes vampires burst into flames in sunlight, sometimes they sparkle.

As our modern lives change, so do the things that scare us ...

and so do our stories.

◆ MEMORY GAME ◆

Look at the pictures. What do you remember reading on the pages where each image appeared?

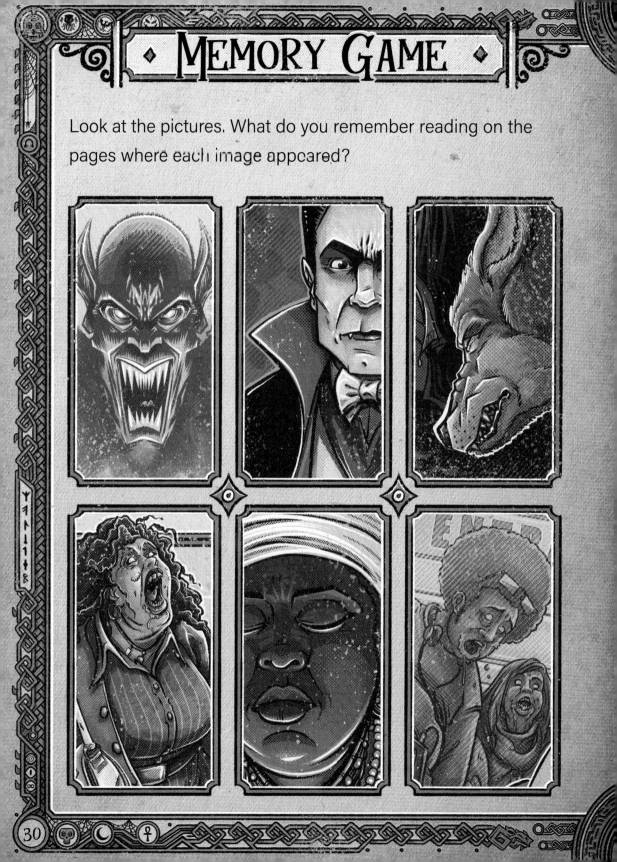

After–Reading Questions

1. Name three countries with myths about vampires.

2. What word means "to come back" in Latin?

3. What disease is related to werewolves?

4. Zombie lore was common in which Caribbean religion?

5. In the modern Hollywood era, what are zombies hungry for?

Activity

If you could travel anywhere in the world, where would you go? Does that place have any monster stories? What monster would you like to meet—or NOT meet—there?!

About the Author

Jen Breach (they/them) grew up in rural Australia where there were no giants or undead, but *plenty* of snakes! Jen has worked as a bagel-baker, a code-breaker, a ticket-taker, and a trouble-maker. They now work as a writer, the best job ever, in Philadelphia, PA.

About the Illustrator

Joshua Janes trained in narrative art at the Joe Kubert School in New Jersey and followed his love of monsters to an illustration career of over 27 years. From his studio in Ohio, his imagination continues to pour forth with the support of his incredible wife, Angie, and their children, Gabi, Bailey, and Cole, along with their bulldog, Pudge.

www.rourkebooks.com

Edited by: Hailey Scragg
Cover and interior illustrations by: Joshua Janes

Library of Congress PCN Data

Mythical Monsters / Jen Breach
(Origin Stories)
ISBN 978-1-73165-732-9 (hard cover) (alk. paper)   ISBN 978-1-73165-745-9 (e-book)
ISBN 978-1-73165-719-0 (soft cover)   ISBN 978-1-73165-758-9 (e-pub)
Library of Congress Control Number: 2023943558
Rourke Educational Media
Printed in the United States of America
01-0152411937